D0811046

★ ★

OREGON

by Liz Sonneborn

GARETH**STEVENS**
GS
P U B L I S H I N G
A Member of the WRC Media Family of Companies

Please visit our web site at: www.garethstevens.com
For a free color catalog describing Gareth Stevens Publishing's
list of high-quality books and multimedia programs, call
1-800-542-2595 (USA) or 1-800-387-3178 (Canada).
Gareth Stevens Publishing's fax: (877) 542-2596.

Library of Congress Cataloging-in-Publication Data

Sonneborn, Liz.
    Oregon / Liz Sonneborn.
       p. cm. — (Portraits of the states)
    Includes bibliographical references and index.
    ISBN-10: 0-8368-4673-7   ISBN-13: 978-0-8368-4673-7 (lib. bdg.)
    ISBN-10: 0-8368-4692-3   ISBN-13: 978-0-8368-4692-8 (softcover)
    1. Oregon—Juvenile literature. I. Title. II. Series.
    F876.3.S67   2006
    979.5—dc22   2005044472

Updated edition reprinted in 2007. First published in 2006 by
Gareth Stevens Publishing
A Weekly Reader Company
1 Reader's Digest Rd.
Pleasantville, NY 10570-7000 USA

Editorial direction: Mark J. Sachner
Project manager: Jonatha A. Brown
Editor: Catherine Gardner
Art direction and design: Tammy West
Picture research: Diane Laska-Swanke
Indexer: Walter Kronenberg
Production: Jessica Morris and Robert Kraus

Picture credits: Cover, p. 18 © James P. Rowan; pp. 4, 20, 24 © Corel; pp. 5, 16
© PhotoDisc; pp. 6, 8 © MPI/Getty Images; p. 9 © North Wind Picture Archives;
p. 10 © Historic Photo Archive/Getty Images; p. 12 US Army Corps of Engineers;
p. 15 © Library of Congress; pp. 22, 26 © John Elk III; p. 25 © Stock Montage/
Getty Images; p. 27 © Harry How/Getty Images; p. 29 © Jeff Belden

Printed in the United States of America

2 3 4 5 6 7 8 9 10 09 08 07

CONTENTS

★ ★

Words that are defined in the Glossary appear
in **bold** the first time they are used in the text.

On the Cover: The Multnomah Falls flow into the Columbia River
Gorge. They are among the highest waterfalls in the United States.

Introduction

Where can you find tall forests and dry, hot deserts? High mountains and ocean beaches? Big cities and small farms? A rose festival and the biggest rodeo in the country? They are all in one state. That state is Oregon.

Oregon is in the northwestern United States. It borders the Pacific Ocean. People from all over the world come to Oregon on vacation. They find plenty to do. Visitors can hike on a trail or climb a mountain. They can windsurf or paddle a kayak down a river.

This state has the deepest lake in the United States. It also has the deepest **gorge** in North America. Oregon has so many wonderful places to explore!

Mount Hood is in the Cascade Mountains. It towers over the Oregon countryside.

The state flag of Oregon.

OREGON FACTS

- Became the 33rd U.S. State: February 14, 1859
- Population (2006): 3,700,758
- Capital: Salem
- Biggest Cities: Portland, Eugene, Salem
- Size: 95,997 square miles (248,632 square kilometers)
- Nickname: The Beaver State
- State Tree: Douglas fir
- State Flower: Oregon grape
- State Animal: Beaver
- State Bird: Western meadowlark

CHAPTER 2

History

People have lived in Oregon for thousands of years. The first people there were Native Americans. More than eighty different groups of Native Americans once made their homes in this area. Some of the groups were the Chinook, Yakima, and Nez Percé. Some groups hunted animals and gathered wild plants. Those near the coast ate seafood.

Newcomers

In the 1500s, white explorers sailed along the Oregon coast. Some of them were from Spain. Others were from England.

A white person first set foot in Oregon in 1792. He was a trader named Robert Gray. He followed the Columbia River and traded with the Native people for animal furs.

The Fur Trade

A group of American explorers reached Oregon in 1805. Meriwether Lewis and William Clark

Sacagawea was a Native American woman. She helped Lewis and Clark speak with other Natives.

led this group. The two men wrote about their trip. People who lived far away read about the rich new land.

Soon, more traders arrived. They came from many places. The traders wanted beaver furs. They wanted the furs because beaver hats were in style. They found lots of beavers in this area.

Jedediah Smith was a fur trapper. In 1828, he left California and went north. He was the first white person to reach Oregon by land.

The State Flag

The beaver has a special place in Oregon history. The state flag honors the beaver. On one side of the flag is the state seal. On the other side is a beaver. It is the only state flag with pictures on both sides.

The **fur trade** did not last long. Trappers killed most of the beavers in the area. By the late 1820s, few beavers were left.

The Oregon Trail

In the 1840s, white settlers began heading west. They had heard that the

Traveling West in the 1840s

Before traveling west, people packed food and supplies. They filled their wagons. Most of the people had to walk. Usually, only children and old people rode in the wagon. They had a bumpy ride on the rough trail. The wagons moved slowly, and the trip took many months. Some settlers did not have enough food. Many of them became sick. About one in ten of them died.

Thousands of settlers traveled to Oregon in wagon trains.

land in Oregon was very **fertile**. A farmer could make a good living there.

Whole families went west in wagons pulled by oxen. Most of them followed the Oregon Trail. It began in the central United States. It was about 2,000 miles (3,219 km) long.

Gold was discovered in California in 1848. People rushed there. They hoped to find gold and get rich.

In the late 1800s, the streets of Portland were lined with shops and full of carriages pulled by horses.

Few people found any gold. Some of them gave up, headed north, and settled in Oregon.

Oregon Grows

For many years, Oregon was claimed by the United States. England and Spain claimed it, too. Later, England and Spain gave up their claims. In 1848, Oregon became a U.S. **territory**. In 1859, it became a state.

Many settlers lived well in Oregon. Some built large farms in the Willamette Valley. The city of Portland grew up there.

Not all of the people lived well, however. The Native Americans suffered because of the settlers. They caught diseases from the settlers. The diseases made them very sick. The settlers also took over their land. Some fought to keep it. By the late 1800s, about half the Native people in the area had died from disease and war. Most of those who survived left the Willamette Valley. The whites forced them to move to **reservations**.

Railroads Reach Oregon

The first railroad reached Portland in 1883. Trains soon began to carry more settlers to the area. The trains carried goods, too. Oregon farmers used the trains to send wheat and other products from their farms to markets far away.

Logging became a big business, too. Oregon soon sold more lumber than any other state.

The Bonneville Dam

In the 1930s, the nation fell on hard times. These years were called the Great Depression. Many people could not find jobs. They could not pay for their food or homes.

The Lash Law

Oregon's settlers often treated African Americans badly. In 1844, slavery was outlawed in Oregon. That same year, however, Oregon passed the Lash Law. This law said that all black people would be whipped twice a year until they moved out. The whites made other unfair laws, too. These laws kept African Americans out of the state for a long time.

These men helped build Portland Railway. They are posing in front of a huge steam shovel.

10

Famous People of Oregon

Abigail Scott Duniway

Born: October 22, 1834, Groveland, Illinois

Died: October 11, 1915, Portland, Oregon

Abigail Scott Duniway raised four children. She helped her husband run a farm, too. One day, her husband had a bad accident. She had to find work to support her family. She started a newspaper in Portland. She put news for women in the paper. At the time, women could not vote. She worked to change the law. In 1912, Duniway became the first woman in the state to register to vote.

The U.S. government tried to help people find jobs. In Oregon, it hired workers to build a **dam** on the Columbia River. Known as the Bonneville Dam, it was used to create electricity from the river water. This electricity helped make Portland a center for building ships. It also lit homes in Oregon and nearby states.

IN OREGON'S HISTORY

The Pendleton Underground

In the 1870s, many Chinese men came to Oregon. They worked on the railroads. White settlers did not welcome the Chinese. The town of Pendleton even passed a law against them. The law said Chinese could not live in the town. The Chinese found a way around the law. They dug tunnels under the town. They built houses and stores and lived under Pendleton! Today, visitors can tour parts of this underground town.

The Bonneville Dam is on the Columbia River. This is how it looks from the air.

Oregon Leads the Way

In the early 1900s, Oregon began bringing new ideas to government. First, it let the state's voters make some laws themselves. This became known as the Oregon System. Then, in 1912, it became one of the first states to let women vote. The state marked another first in the 1990s. It held a statewide election by mail. In 2000, people in Oregon voted for president with mail-in ballots.

Oregon has led the nation in other ways, too. It has worked for years to protect its **natural resources**. It was one of the first states to start recycling. The people of Oregon try hard to take care of their beautiful state.

FUN FACTS

First Facts

In 1991, Barbara Roberts became Oregon's first female governor. The next year, James A. Hill Jr. was elected state treasurer. He was the first African American to hold a statewide office in Oregon.

1579	English explorers sail along the Oregon coast.
1792	American trader Robert Gray explores the Columbia River.
1805	American explorers Meriwether Lewis and William Clark canoe along the Columbia River.
1828	Jedediah Smith travels overland from California to Oregon.
1844	Slavery is outlawed in Oregon, but the "lash laws," designed to scare African Americans out of Oregon, are passed the same year.
1846	England gives up its claims to Oregon.
1848	Oregon Territory is established.
1859	Oregon becomes the thirty-third U.S. state.
1883	The first railroad to Oregon is completed.
1912	Oregon women gain the right to vote.
1938	Construction of the Bonneville Dam is finished.
1993	Oregon holds the first statewide vote-by-mail election.
2005	Oregon celebrates the two-hundredth anniversary of Lewis and Clark's journey along the Columbia River.

People

Native Americans were the first people in Oregon. In the 1840s, white settlers arrived. They brought diseases and war. Many Natives died or were killed. Others were forced to leave their lands. Today, many Natives in the state live on reservations.

From Many Places

The first white settlers in Oregon had ties to Europe. Their relatives came from countries such as England, Germany, and

Hispanics: In the 2000 U.S. Census, 8.0 percent of the people in Oregon called themselves Latino or Hispanic. Most of them or their relatives came from places where Spanish is spoken. They may come from different racial backgrounds.

The People of Oregon

Total Population 3,700,758

White
86.6%

Native American
1.3 %

Black or African American 1.6 %

Asian
3.0%

Other
7.5 %

Percentages are based on the 2000 Census.

Scotland. Most of these settlers became farmers.

In the late 1800s, other people arrived. Some were from Italy and Greece. Others were from China. These people helped build the state's first railroad. Most of them made their homes in Portland.

Japanese people came to the state in the early 1900s. Many worked on small farms. In the early 1940s, the United States went to war against Japan. During the war, Japanese Americans were forced to leave their homes in Oregon. The U.S. government sent them to camps for most of the war. These people had done nothing wrong. Even so, they lost their homes and their goods. In the late 1900s, the government admitted that it had treated them unfairly.

Newcomers still arrive in Oregon every day. Some come from other states. Others come from different countries such as Mexico

The skyscrapers of Portland tower over the Willamette River. Portland is the busiest port in the northwestern United States.

and China. Today, less than half of the people in Oregon were born in the state.

For years, strict laws kept most African Americans out of Oregon. Even today, few black people live in the state. They make up less than 2 percent of the population.

Where They Live

About 3.6 million people live in Oregon today. Most of them are city people. About seven in ten people live in or near cities. Portland is the biggest city in the state.

Most of the state's cities and big towns are in the Willamette Valley. This area is home to more than 70 percent of the people in

Oregon. The valley is getting crowded.

Fewer people live in small towns and villages. They are scattered around the state. Some people live on farms. Few people live in the state's desert areas.

Religion and Education

Most people in Oregon are Christians. They include Baptists, Lutherans, and Methodists. Other people are Jews, Muslims, and Buddhists. A few practice Native American religions.

Oregon's first schools opened in the 1800s. Christian **missionaries** ran these schools. They taught Native Americans about their religion.

The oldest university in the state is Willamette University in Salem. It opened in 1842. Oregon

Famous People of Oregon

Chief Joseph

Born: About 1840, Wallowa Valley, Oregon Territory

Died: September 21, 1904, Colville Reservation, Washington

Chief Joseph was a Native American. He was the leader of the Nez Percé. He wanted to live in peace with the white people. In 1876, war broke out, but Chief Joseph did not want to fight the whites. He and his people fled toward Canada. The U.S. Army followed them. Many Nez Percé died of hunger during the chase. Finally, the army caught the Nez Percé. Chief Joseph gave up. He said, "I will fight no more forever."

has many universities today. The biggest is the University of Portland.

The Land

The land in Oregon changes from place to place. Some places have snow-capped mountains. Others have beautiful ocean beaches. Still others have dusty deserts. Few states have so many kinds of landscapes.

The Oregon Coast

Western Oregon borders the Pacific Ocean. Along the coast are rocky cliffs and sandy beaches. This part of the state has many rivers. They include the Columbia, Rogue, and Chetco Rivers.

The Willamette Valley

East of the coast is the Willamette Valley. This valley is 115 miles (185 km) long and 30 miles (48 km)

FUN FACTS

Crater Lake

One of the most beautiful places in the Cascades is Crater Lake. It is more than seven thousand years old. This lake was formed from a volcano. When the volcano erupted, it left behind a giant hole, called a crater. Water filled the crater, forming the lake. It is 1,932 feet (589 meters) deep. It is the deepest lake in the United States. The only national park in Oregon is at Crater Lake.

Blue sky and fluffy white clouds are reflected in the waters of Crater Lake.

OREGON

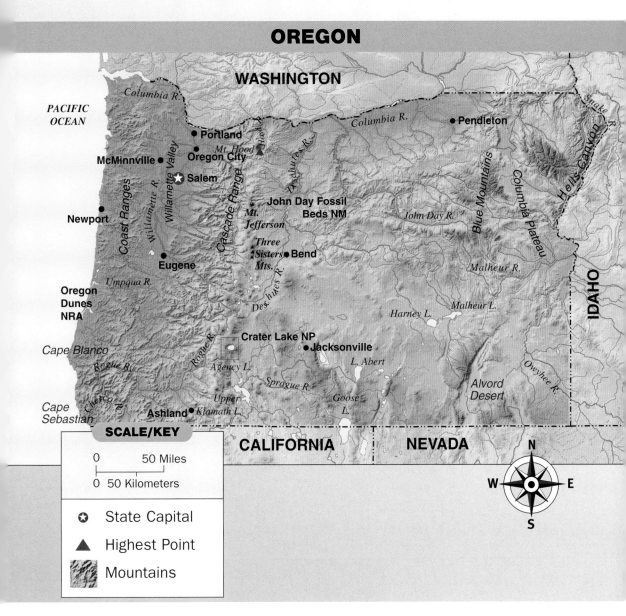

WASHINGTON

PACIFIC OCEAN

Columbia R.

Columbia R.

Snake R.

• Pendleton

Hells Canyon

• Portland

Mt. Hood

Deschutes R.

Blue Mountains

Columbia Plateau

IDAHO

McMinnville •

• Oregon City

Coast Ranges

Willamette R.

Willamette Valley

Cascade Range

☆ Salem

John Day Fossil Beds NM

Mt. Jefferson

John Day R.

Newport •

Three Sisters Mts.

• Bend

Deschutes R.

Malheur R.

Eugene •

Oregon Dunes NRA

Umpqua R.

Malheur L.

Deschutes R.

Harney L.

Cape Blanco

Rogue R.

Rogue R.

Crater Lake NP

• Jacksonville

Agency L.

L. Abert

Owyhee R.

Chetco R.

Sprague R.

Goose L.

Alvord Desert

Cape Sebastian

Ashland •

Upper Klamath L.

SCALE/KEY

0   50 Miles

0   50 Kilometers

CALIFORNIA | **NEVADA**

N
W   E
S

⊗   State Capital

▲   Highest Point

🏔   Mountains

---

wide. The land is rich, and the weather is mild. The Willamette River winds through this area.

The city of Portland is on the Willamette River.

This part of the state is a popular place to live.

The Cascades

East of the Willamette Valley are the Cascade Mountains. These mountains stretch across Oregon from north to south.

Several extinct volcanoes are in the Cascades. One is Mount Hood, the highest point in the state. It rises 11,239 feet (3,426 m) into the air. People in Portland, can see Mount Hood on a clear day.

Some people climb the Cascade Mountains. Some of them even reach the top of Mount Hood. When it snows, people ski down the slopes.

The Plateau and Great Basin

In eastern Oregon lies the Columbia **Plateau**. Rolling hills cover this

Oregon's mountains are home to elk and other animals.

Major Rivers

Columbia River
1,214 miles (1,953 km) long

Snake River
1,038 miles (1,670 km) long

Willamette River
300 miles (485 km) long

dry area. Farmers grow wheat there.

Farther southeast is the Great Basin. This is a large desert area. It makes up about one-fourth of the state. Rain rarely falls there, so the land is very dry. The weather can be quite hot.

At other times, however, it is icy cold.

On Oregon's eastern edge is the Snake River. It runs through a deep gorge called Hells Canyon. The canyon is 7,900 feet (2,408 m) deep. It is the deepest gorge in North America.

Malheur Lake lies in the Great Basin. It is the state's second-largest lake. Some years, little rain falls, and the lake dries up. Then, it no longer looks like a lake. It looks like a giant hole of mud.

Plants and Animals

Forests cover more than 40 percent of the land in the state. Other plants also grow wild. Colorful wildflowers bloom in the country. The moist air in Portland is perfect for roses. Portland is nicknamed the "City of Roses."

FUN FACTS

Environment and Business

Some people in Oregon are **environmentalists**. They work to protect the state's forests and rivers. They try to save the wild plants, fish, and animals. Environmentalists do not want more dams on Oregon's rivers. Dams make it hard for salmon to swim. Other people feel differently. They want more dams to make more electricity for businesses. These two groups are trying to work out their differences.

Many animals live in Oregon. The beaver is the state animal. It is the largest rodent in North America. Larger wild animals, such as deer, elk, and antelope, live there, too. Bears and cougars roam in the mountains. In some spots in the state, bald eagles fly overhead.

21

Economy

The people of Oregon have long made their living off the land. Native Americans hunted animals and traded furs. Settlers farmed crops and cut lumber. Today, many people still make a living from natural resources.

Farms and Forests

Thousands of people work on farms. Some farmers raise beef cattle. Others raise cows to produce milk. Farmers grow nuts, fruits, and vegetables. Wheat is a big crop. Oregon is the top grower of hazelnuts and blackberries in the nation.

Water is precious to Oregon farmers. Almost half of them use **irrigation** to water their fields.

Farmers in the Willamette Valley grow many crops, including wheat.

Some people make money from the forests. They cut down trees for lumber or grow Christmas trees. More lumber and Christmas trees come from Oregon than any other state.

Fishing and Factories

Fishing is important in Oregon, too. Snapper and sole are the biggest catches.

Factories in this state make many products from wood. These products include paper, plywood, and cardboard. In the Willamette Valley, some companies build computers. This industry is growing quickly in Oregon.

Ships carry goods along the Columbia River system. It is the second-busiest shipping system in the nation. Portland is the biggest **port** in the Northwest.

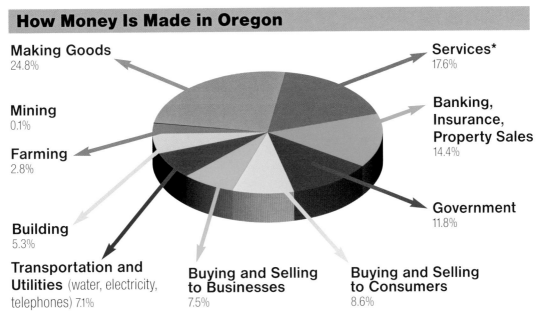

How Money Is Made in Oregon

Making Goods
24.8%

Mining
0.1%

Farming
2.8%

Building
5.3%

Transportation and Utilities (water, electricity, telephones) 7.1%

Buying and Selling to Businesses
7.5%

Buying and Selling to Consumers
8.6%

Services*
17.6%

Banking, Insurance, Property Sales
14.4%

Government
11.8%

* Services include jobs in hotels, restaurants, auto repair, medicine, teaching, and entertainment.

Government

Oregon's government has three parts, or branches. They are the executive, legislative, and judicial branches.

State **officials** work in Salem. This city is the state capital.

Executive Branch

The governor heads the executive branch. This branch makes sure state laws are carried out. Five other elected officials work in the executive branch.

Oregon's governor and other elected officials work in the state capitol.

Herbert Hoover was the president of the United States from 1929 until 1933. He was raised in Newberg, Oregon.

Legislative Branch

The legislative branch is called the Legislative Assembly. It includes the Senate and House of Representatives. They work together to make new laws.

Judicial Branch

Judges and courts make up the judicial branch. Judges and courts may decide whether people who have been accused of committing crimes are guilty.

Local Government

Oregon has thirty-six counties. Teams of two to five people run twenty-four of counties. Courts of one judge and two other people run the other twelve.

OREGON'S STATE GOVERNMENT

Executive		Legislative		Judicial	
Office	**Length of Term**	**Body**	**Length of Term**	**Court**	**Length of Term**
Governor	4 years	Senate (30 members)	4 years	Supreme (7 justices)	6 years
Secretary of State	4 years	House of Representatives (60 members)	2 years	Appeals (10 judges)	6 years

Things to See and Do

It is easy to have fun in Oregon. Each part of this state has things to do. Oregon's rivers and ocean are great for water sports. People swim, fish, canoe, and windsurf on the water.

The state's forests attract campers and hikers. The state has hundreds of places to pitch a tent. Hikers often spot wild animals. Sometimes, they even spy a bear.

The Cascade Mountains are popular. In winter, visitors ski. In summer, they ride mountain bikes. Mountain climbers also go to the Cascades.

Waves wash onto the rocky shore of Ecola State Park.

Portland is one of the best cities for bicycling. It has 200 miles (322 km) of bike paths. Many people ride bikes to work.

Watching Sports

People in Oregon do not just play sports. They love to watch sports, too. They especially like basketball. Their professional team is the Portland Trail Blazers.

College football is also popular. Teams from the University of Oregon and Oregon State draw big crowds.

People also enjoy college track-and-field meets. Mary Decker Slaney and Steve Prefontaine are famous Oregon track athletes.

Places to Visit

Oregon's cities and towns have lots of things to do. To watch plays, people often go to

Oregon's Bison

Visitors to eastern Oregon can see bison. They are the biggest mammals in North America. A ranch in Oregon raises bison for meat. Each animal has lots of meat. An average bison weighs more than 1,000 pounds (454 kilograms)!

Players from Notre Dame try to catch a member of the Oregon State Beavers football team.

Famous People of Oregon

Beverly Cleary

Born: April 12, 1916, McMinnville, Oregon

Beverly Cleary is a famous author. She writes books for children. As a little girl, she lived on a farm in Oregon. Then, her family moved to Portland. She wrote about her life in *A Girl from Yamhill*. She has written more than thirty books. Two of her famous books are *Henry Huggins* and *Beezus and Ramona*. Her books have sold more than ten million copies.

Ashland. This city has nine theater groups.

Jacksonville is also fun to visit. It was built in the 1850s. Even today, some streets still are lined with old buildings. Going to this city is like taking a trip back in time.

Many cities and towns have museums. The High Desert Museum is in the town of Bend. It shows how animals and plants live in the desert. The Oregon Coast Aquarium is in Newport. The whale in the movie *Free Willy* once lived there.

In Jacksonville, the Catalogue House is an interesting spot to see. Jeremiah Nunan built it in 1893. He ordered the house in pieces from a catalog. The pieces came by train from Tennessee. They filled fourteen train cars. It took six months to put them together.

Famous People of Oregon

Linus Pauling

Born: February 28, 1901, Portland, Oregon

Died: August 19, 1994, Big Sur, California

Linus Pauling was a great scientist. He studied chemistry. He made many discoveries that helped doctors understand more about illnesses. He was also famous for speaking out against nuclear weapons. He won two Nobel Prizes. One of them was for his work in chemistry. The other one was for his efforts to spread peace.

Festival Fun

Special events also bring people to the state. Portland holds its Rose Festival each year. More than two million people attend it.

Pendleton hosts the biggest rodeo in the nation. Every September, people watch cowhands rope and herd cattle.

Another fun event is Sandcastle Day. On this day, thousands go to Cannon Beach. There, people compete to build the best castle out of sand.

Native Americans hold powwows. At these big events, they celebrate their **culture**.

Cowboys rope cattle before large crowds at the Pendleton Round-Up.

culture — the ways of life for certain countries or groups of people, which includes their history, art, and customs

dam — a barrier built across a waterway to slow down water flow

environmentalists — people who work to protect land and air from harm

fertile — rich in materials needed to grow plants

fur trade — the exchange of animal furs for other goods

gorge — a deep valley with steep, rocky sides

irrigation — using ditches to send water from a river or stream to a field

missionaries — people who spread a religion

natural resources — water, timber, and other valuable material found in nature

officials — people who hold important jobs in an organization, such as a government

plateau — an area of land that is high and flat

port — a city with a harbor where ships dock and load or unload goods

reservations — areas of land set aside by the government for a special purpose

territory — an area that belongs to a country

trading post — a building in the wilderness where people exchanged goods, such as furs, for food and supplies

Books

B Is for Beaver: An Oregon Alphabet. Marie and Roland Smith (Sleeping Bear Press)

Chief Joseph. Rachel A. Koestler-Grack (Heinemann)

The Columbia River. Rivers of North America (series). Tom Jackson (Gareth Stevens)

Oregon. This Land Is Your Land (series). Ann Heinrichs (Compass Point Books)

Oregon Facts and Symbols. States and Their Symbols (series). Emily McAuliffe (Capstone)

The Oregon Trail. We the People (series). Jean F. Blashfield (Compass Point Books)

People of the Northwest and Subarctic. Linda Thompson (Rourke)

Web Sites

Lewis and Clark
www.pbs.org/lewisandclark

Oregon Blue Book for kids
bluebook.state.or.us/kids/index.htm

The Oregon Trail
www.isu.edu/~trinmich/Oregontrail.html

INDEX